# WHAT MRS. FISHER KNOWS ABOUT OLD SOUTHERN COOKING: SOUPS, PICKLES, PRESERVES, ETC.

## By ABBY FISHER

*Awarded Two Medals at the San Francisco Mechanics'
Institute Fair, 1880, for best Pickles and Sauces and
best assortment of Jellies and Preserves.*

DIPLOMA AWARDED AT SACRAMENTO STATE FAIR, 1879.

What Mrs. Fisher Knows About Old Southern Cooking: Soups, Pickles,
    Preserves, etc.
By Abby Fisher

Print ISBN 13: 978-1-4209-6998-6
eBook ISBN 13: 978-1-4209-6999-3

Cover Image: a detail of "Nature Morte", by Bernhard Dorotheus
Folkestad, (oil on canvas) / Photo © O. Vaering / Bridgeman Images.

Please visit *www.digireads.com*

# CONTENTS

## Preface and Apology.

The publication of a book on my knowledge and experience of Southern Cooking, Pickle and Jelly Making, has been frequently asked of me by my lady friends and patrons in San Francisco and Oakland, and also by ladies of Sacramento during the State Fair in 1879. Not being able to read or write myself, and my husband also having been without the advantages of an education—upon whom would devolve the writing of the book at my dictation—caused me to doubt whether I would be able to present a work that would give perfect satisfaction. But, after due consideration, I concluded to bring forward a book of my knowledge—based on an experience of upwards of thirty-five years—in the art of cooking Soups, Gumbos, Terrapin Stews, Meat Stews, Baked and Roast Meats, Pastries, Pies and Biscuits, making Jellies, Pickles, Sauces, Ice-Creams and Jams, preserving Fruits, etc. The book will be found a complete instructor, so that a child can understand it and learn the art of cooking.

Respectfully,
MRS. ABBY FISHER,
Late of Mobile, Ala.

I take pleasure in referring, by permission, to the following of my friends, namely:

WM. F. BLOOD: 415 California Street, San Francisco
E. M. MILES: 413 Montgomery Street, San Francisco
WM. O. GOULD: 512 California Street, San Francisco
MRS. CHARLES S. NEALE: 1814 Sutter Street, San Francisco
MRS. JOHN HARROLD: 416 Chestnut Street, San Francisco
MRS. W. H. GLASCOCK: Oakland
MRS. G. H. COY: 431 Geary Street, San Francisco
MRS. JOHN C. FALLS: San Francisco
Mrs. Louis H. Vanschaick: 129 Page Street, San Francisco

# WHAT MRS. FISHER KNOWS

## ABOUT

## OLD SOUTHERN COOKING.

### *1. Maryland Beat Biscuit.*

Take one quart of flour, add one tea spoonful of salt, one tablespoonful of lard, half tablespoonful of butter. Dry rub the lard and butter into the flour until well creamed; add your water gradually in mixing so as to make dough stiff, then put the dough on pastry board and beat until perfectly moist and light. Roll out the dough to thickness of third of an inch. Have your stove hot and bake quickly. To make more add twice the quantity.

### *2. Egg Rolls.*

One quart of flour, half tablespoonful of butter, two eggs lightly beat, half tea-cup of sweet yeast, half tea-cup of water, one teaspoonful of salt. Mix as a sponge, about 10 o'clock at night, for breakfast; put to rise until morning. With dry flour knead the sponge, not too stiff; make off rolls, put to rise in baking pan, then have oven hot and bake slowly. When rolls are done, put them in a napkin until sent to table.

### *3. Breakfast Cream Cake.*

Four eggs beat light, one gill of cream to a tea-cup of sweet milk, one pint of flour, sifted, half teaspoonful of salt; mix cream, milk, and eggs together, well stirred, then add flour gradually until thoroughly mixed. Have your baking cups hot when put to bake. Requires ten minutes to bake in hot oven.

### *4. Waffles for Breakfast.*

Two eggs beat light, one pint of sour milk, to one and a half pint of flour, one teaspoonful of soda sifted with the flour, one tablespoonful of butter, teaspoonful of salt, well mixed, and then add the eggs. Always have your irons perfectly hot and well greased., In baking, melt butter before mixing in flour. Place them in a covered dish and butter them on sending to the table.

### 5. Flannel Cake.

One quart of flour, quarter tea-cup of yeast, make into a batter, with one teaspoonful of salt; make up over night and put to rise. Just before baking on a nicely greased griddle, for breakfast, add one level teaspoonful of soda, and stir it well into the batter.

### 6. Sally Lund.

One quart of flour, quarter pound of butter, perfectly rubbed into the flour while dry, one teaspoonful of salt, five eggs beat very light, half tea-cup of milk to quarter tea-cup of yeast; add all to the flour, and stir the whole together as you would pound cake, and put to rise at 10 o'clock at night; next morning beat over until light as cake and put in warm place to rise a second time, after which bake as carefully as baking pound cake. Bake in the pan it rises in the second time. Just grease the pan before putting to rise the second time.

### 7. Breakfast Corn Bread.

One tea-cup of rice boiled nice and soft, to one and a half tea-cupful of corn meal mixed together, then stir the whole until light; one teaspoonful of salt, one tablespoonful of lard or butter, three eggs, half tea-cup of sweet milk. The rice must be mixed into the meal while hot; can be baked either in muffin cups or a pan.

### 8. Corn Egg Bread.

Two eggs, one pint of meal, half pint of sour milk, one teaspoonful of soda,—beat eggs very light,—one tablespoonful of melted lard or butter, mix all together, well stirred or beaten. Bake in an ordinary pan.

### 9. Plantation Corn Bread or Hoe Cake.

Half tablespoonful of lard to a pint of meal, one tea-cup of boiling water; stir well and bake on a hot griddle. Sift in meal one teaspoonful of soda.

### 10. Light Bread.

Half yeast cake to two quarts of flour, teaspoonful of salt, one dessertspoonful of butter or lard. Dissolve yeast in warm water; make up over night at 10 o'clock; make dough soft and spongy, and set to rise in a warm place. Next morning work the dough over until it becomes perfectly light, adding flour so as to keep it from sticking to the hands, then put to rise in your baking pan, and when it rises bake in a hot oven until thoroughly done.

### 11. Beefsteak—Broiled.

Which should not be broiled until a few minutes before meal time: First, have the gridiron perfectly hot, then lay the steak on the iron while hot, the iron being over hot coals. Let the steak be on the iron about two minutes the first time you lay it on the iron, turning it over about once. In a minute remove from iron to a platter or pan and stick it through and through with a fork, so as to let the blood run out. Then place the steak back on the hot iron, turning it over as before; then take off iron, salt and pepper it and baste with butter; then lay it back on gridiron, turning it over for about two minutes; then lay in a dish, dress with butter and send to the table. A steak an inch and one-half thick may require twelve minutes to broil, turning it over every three minutes. A steak broiled in this style is very sweet and nice.

### 12. Lamb or Mutton Chops.

Will take five minutes to broil, and must observe the same directions you have in the beefsteak

### 13. Pork Steak or Chops.

Should be broiled in the same way as the beefsteak, except that about eight to ten minutes should broil them, as pork must be well done.

### 14. Venison—Broiled.

Pepper and salt before putting it on the gridiron, but remove it every two or three minutes from the iron and baste with butter. When you want deviled venison, use a little mustard mixed with wine (claret). Should you like your venison tart or a little acid, baste with currant jelly.

### 15. Roast Venison.

First stuff the meat before roasting; make stuffing of bread crumbs browned; season stuffing with butter, salt, onions (grated), pork or ham chopped fine. When it is put into the oven, baste well with butter or lard, and while cooking notice and continue to baste until done. Two hours are sufficient, with a hot fire, to cook this roast. To make your gravy, brown a tablespoonful of flour in your pan from which you take the roast, add a little water, stir with spoon slowly until well done. You can make your gravy thick by the use of a very little water. If you do not like onions, use a little green or dry thyme.

### 16. Roast Beef.

Should be well cooked outside and rare on the inside. The oven should bake on bottom and top. If it gets too hot on either top or bottom, shut the damper slightly off. A five-pound roast should cook in half an hour, and a ten-pound one in one hour. Season roast with salt and pepper before putting it to cook, baste it with lard or butter before putting in stove, and while cooking baste with the juice that comes out of the meat every two or three minutes until done.

### 17. Roast Lamb.

Prepare in the same way as the roast beef, except the lamb should be well done. In a hot oven, one hour is necessary to cook the lamb. Mint sauce for roast lamb: Chop tender mint very fine, put cold water or vinegar, one tablespoonful of vinegar to three of water, and a little sugar according to taste.

### 18. Roast Pork.

To be seasoned with salt and pepper before being cooked, and in cooking baste with the gravy that comes from the meat. Must be cooked with a fast fire. To make the gravy, take one tablespoonful of flour browned in the pan and stir in a little water.

### 19. Roast Pig.

Examine when it comes from the butcher and see that it is completely cleaned. The pig should be roasted the same way you would a turkey well done. For the stuffing take a loaf and one-half of baker's bread cut thin, fry the bread in butter or lard and mash it well; season it with salt and pepper according to taste, using a little red pepper. Then stuff the pig putting an apple in its mouth. Put it in the pan and baste with lard, then put it to roast, and while it is cooking keep basting it every five or ten minutes until it is cooked; you can tell when it is perfectly done by a fork passing through it easily. To make the gravy for the pig—After it is cooked, take about a tablespoonful of flour and put it in the pan where you cooked your roast and brown well on the stove, then add a little water; stir till it commences to get thick. A little onion in your stuffing is good. [See No. 21.]

### 20. Roast Veal.

Use crackers for your stuffing. Slice an opening in the veal in five or six different places, and fill each one with the stuffing. Season the stuffing with salt, pepper, butter, and a little sage. You can tell when it is done by a fork passing through easily. Baste the roast while cooking with the essence that comes from the meat. Baste it with lard or butter when first put to cook. Use flour for making gravy, same as directed in other roasts.

### 21. Roast Turkey.

First cleanse well and take the craw from the turkey. Make stuffing of light bread chopped fine, season with butter, pepper and salt; then stuff the body completely full, also where the craw was. Put in pan and baste with butter or lard, and put to roast. While cooking, keep basting it with the juice that comes from the turkey. When it is cooked take a tablespoonful of flour and brown it in the pan, then add a little water and stir for the gravy.

### 22. Roast Chicken.

The same as for turkey.

### 23. Roast Birds.

In the same way.

### 24. Quails.

When roasted, make nice toast, butter it nice and send quails to table on the toast. Do not forget to baste all game and fowls while cooking, so as to make them juicy. Make stuffing same as for chicken.

### 25. Domestic Duck.

Bake or roast in the same manner you do a turkey, and have it well cooked. Make stuffing of bread, like that prepared for turkey, with salt, pepper, butter or lard. Baste while cooking.

### 26. Wild Duck.

Should not be stuffed, but cleaned well and seasoned with pepper and salt, inside and outside, and put into a hot oven. Ten minutes will cook it.

### 27. Meat Stews or Entrees.

Cut your meat into inch pieces and put into a saucepan; season with salt, pepper, and butter or lard. Put one pint of water to a pound of meat. One hour will cook, unless very young, when less time is sufficient. Add onions if liked.

### 28. Lamb Croquettes.

Boil lamb till thoroughly done, then cut into small pieces taking all sinews and gristle out, and put into a chopping tray; grate onion in it to suit your taste, also grate two or three sour pickles in it; then chop the whole up very fine indeed. Season with salt and pepper. Add one and one half boiled Irish potatoes to one pound of lamb mashed to the fine meal while hot; thoroughly mix together with the hand. Make into small cakes, oblong style; then take two eggs and beat them very light, dip the cakes into the egg, and then roll into powdered crackers. Have fat very hot and put them into it, and let them fry quick till brown.

### 29. Chicken Croquettes.

Boil chicken very tender, pick to pieces, take all gristle out, then chop fine. Beat two eggs for one chicken and mix into meat; season with pepper and salt; make into cakes oblong shaped; powder crackers and roll them into the powder, after dipping them into two eggs beaten moderately well. Then have your lard very hot, and fry just before sending them to the table.

### 30. Crab Croquettes.

Have crabs well boiled in salt and water, then pick them clean from the shell; chop fine; take the large end of a piece of celery and grate into the crab; chop with crab a small piece of onion fine; mix half a tea-cup of fine powdered cracker into crab; season with pepper and salt, also the least bit of fine red pepper, as crabs should be seasoned high to be nice. Have your lard hot, and fry just before wanted at table. Beat two eggs, dip croquettes in the egg, roll in powdered crackers before frying; make them oblong shaped.

### 31. Meat Croquettes.

You can make croquettes from any kind of meat you like from the directions given for the lamb croquettes, such as veal, except make veal into cakes as you would a biscuit, round. You need not use onions unless you like, but always salt and pepper.

### 32. Veal or Lamb Vigareets.

To be made the same way, to-wit: Boil meat rare done, pick all gristle out, grate as much onion in the chopped meat as you like. Take half the quantity of brains that comes in one head (calf or lamb), scald them, pick all the skin from them; mix then with the meat, one-half of a nutmeg grated, pepper and salt; season high and fry the same as other croquettes. Make a gravy of cream and pour on vigareets just as going to table. Making gravy: Put sweet cream into a clean vessel, put over steam until hot, add a very little pepper and salt, then chop some fresh parsley fine and sprinkle it over vigareets while on dish. Make oblong cakes.

### 33. Liver Croquettes.

Made of lamb or veal liver. One pound of liver to a quarter of a pound of suet, part boil, chop both separately very fine; pick all strings out of suet, then add suet and liver together, a small piece of onion, grated, salt and pepper; season high. Beat one egg light and mix well with hand, roll in powdered cracker, fry in hot lard or butter, garnish dish with parsley and send to table.

### 34. Oyster Croquettes.

Chop the quantity of oysters you want for the dinner in the following manner: Chop very fine one dozen oysters, take one boiled potato and mash hot into the fine oysters; take the yolk of one egg only, mix well into the oysters and season with pepper and salt to taste; then roll them, after making into oblong cakes, in powdered crackers; have your fat very hot, and fry quick and send to table.

### 35. Fish Croquettes.

One pound of boiled fish to one and a half potatoes, chop a small piece of onion fine and mix with fish; season with pepper and salt to your taste; make them out in cakes like the other croquettes, roll them in dry corn meal, fry in hot fat and send to table.

### 36. Fricasseed Chicken.

Chicken must be tender and well cleaned inside. Singe all pin feathers off over the fire. Boil two eggs hard, take the yolks and rub fine into one tablespoonful of butter, then add one tablespoonful of corn starch dissolved into the least bit of water; add all together, well mixed and free from lumps. Have your chicken cut up before boiling, and stir the fricassee into the chicken just before sending to table. Season with salt and pepper while cooking.

### 37. Fried Chicken.

Cut the chicken up, separating every joint, and wash clean. Salt and pepper it, and roll into flour well. Have your fat very hot, and drop the pieces into it, and let them cook brown. The chicken is done when the fork passes easily into it. After the chicken is all cooked, leave a little of the hot fat in the skillet; then take a tablespoonful of dry flour and brown it in the fat, stirring it around, then pour water in and stir till the gravy is as thin as soup.

### 38. Beef Soup.

Six pounds of meat to two and one-half gallons of water. Boil to one gallon and one-half; then strain all meat out from the bouillon. Season with pepper and salt.

### 39. Ox-Tail Soup.

Can be made from the same bouillon of beef as seen in No. 38, in the following manner. Take two quarts of bouillon to two ox-tails; boil down to three pints. You can put in either ochre or vermicelli. Season with salt and pepper. Skim all grease off while boiling. Have the butcher unjoint the ox-tail.

### 40. Calf's Head Soup.

Let the butcher open the head wide. Take the brains from it and lay into clean water with a little salt. Leave the tongue in the head when put on to boil; when the tongue is tenderly boiled or done, take it out of the pot and let it get cold for making tongue salad. Two gallons of water to, a calf's head; boil to one gallon; strain it off clear for soup to one dozen guests. Take two quarts of this liquid and put to boil; two tablespoonfuls of flour and brown it; one tablespoonful of butter; rub into the brown flour till it comes to a cream, then add to the soup gradually, and stir well while adding. Season with salt and pepper, and a little red pepper. While cooking, boil a small piece of thyme and the half of an ordinary sized onion tied tight in a clean linen rag, and to be taken out of soup when done. One teaspoonful of mustard mixed with one tablespoonful of wine, to be put into the tureen before pouring in the soup hot, also one glass of sherry wine. Pick all skin from brains; beat two eggs light and add to the brains, then beat the eggs and brains together to a batter; take one-quarter tea cup of powdered cracker, one tablespoonful of flour added to the brains and egg batter well beaten together. Then make this brain batter in cake the size of a hickory nut, and fry them brown in hot fat just before taking up soup, and send to table on separate dish. Serve them with the soup, two cakes to a plate of soup.

P. S.—Chop parsley very fine, and boil it into the soup. You will find the calf's head soup the most delicious soup in the cookery. Study the recipe and remember it well.

### 41. Mock Turtle Soup.

Follow the same directions given for calf's head soup. Prepare your calf's head in the same way exactly. Use for flavor half of a lemon sliced, and put in tureen and pour hot soup on. Instead of brain-balls or cakes, make a forced meat of boiled ham chopped very fine with the yolk of a hardboiled egg; season with black pepper. Make balls the size of a hickory nut and fry in hot butter. Send to table in separate dish, serving one ball to a plate of soup. Use beef in place of ham if liked best.

### 42. Green Turtle Soup.

To two pounds of turtle add two quarts of water, put to boil an a slow fire and cook down to three pints. Season while boiling with pepper and salt to taste. Take three hard boiled eggs, slice very thin and lay in tureen; slice one-fourth of a lemon and put in tureen also. Then pour in tureen one gill of sherry wine. Then pour on hot soup and send to table. The above quantity will make soup for one dozen guests. If there are more to serve, increase the quantity.

### 43. Oyster Gumbo Soup.

Take an old chicken, cut into small pieces, salt and black pepper. Dip it well in flour, and put it on to fry, over a slow fire, till brown; don't let it burn. Cut half of a small onion very fine and sprinkle on chicken while frying. Then place chicken in soup pot, add two quarts water and let it boil to three pints. Have one quart of fresh oysters with all the liquor that belongs to them, and before dishing up soup, add oysters and let come to a boil the second time, then stir into soup one tablespoonful of gumbo quickly. Dish up and send to table. Have parsley chopped very fine and put in tureen on dishing up soup. Have dry boiled rice to go to table with gumbo in separate dish. Serve one tablespoonful of rice to a plate of gumbo.

### 44. Ochre Gumbo.

Get a beef shank, have it cracked and put to boil in one gallon of water. Boil to half a gallon, then strain and put back on fire. Cut ochre in small pieces and put in soup; don't put in any ends of ochre. Season with salt and pepper while cooking. Stir it occasionally and keep it from burning. To be sent to table with dry boiled rice. Never stir rice while boiling. Season rice always with salt when it is first put on to cook, and do not have too much water in rice while boiling.

### 45. Old Fashioned Turnip Soup.

Take two pounds veal bones to half a gallon of water, and boil to one quart. Put turnips and bones on to boil together, then strain the liquor off and send to table hot. Season while cooking with pepper and salt.

### 46. Chicken Soup for the Sick.

Take an old chicken and put on with one gallon of water; boil down to half a gallon. Take the yolks of two eggs, tie them up in a clean cloth with a little thyme and put in the soup after you have strained the meat from it, and put back to boil till down to three pints. Dish up and send to table hot. Season with salt and pepper to taste.

### 47. Corn and Tomato Soup.

Take a fresh beef bone, put on to boil with one gallon of water, and when boiling skim the grease off. Cut corn from cob and scald tomatoes with boiling water. Skin them and put both vegetables into soup, the corn ten minutes before dinner. Cut tomatoes in small pieces and let them boil in soup at least one hour.

### 48. Pastry for making Pies of all kinds.

One pound of flour nicely sifted to quarter pound of butter and one quarter pound of lard, one teaspoonful of salt, fine, mixed in flour while dry; then with your hands rub the butter and lard into the flour until thoroughly mixed, then add enough cold water and mix with your hands so as to make pastry hold together, be sure not have it too wet; sprinkle flour very lightly on pastry board, and roll pastry out to the thickness of an egg-shell for the top of fruit, and that for the bottom of fruit must be thin as paper. In rolling pastry, roll to and from you; you don't want more than ten minutes to make pastry.

### 49. Preparing the Fruit for Pies.

One gill of water to four pounds rhubarb; first peel the rhubarb; sweeten to taste while cooking, and put into pastry when cold.

Prepare apples same way; season with cinnamon.

Peaches the same way; season with cinnamon.

### 50. Lemon Pies.

Take four eggs, one tablespoonful of butter to one and a half tea-cup of powdered sugar, rub butter and sugar together until a cream, then add the yolks of the eggs to butter and sugar, and beat until light; beat the white of the egg until perfectly light, and add to the others. Take two lemons, roll them with your hands, on board until soft, then grate peel of lemons and put into preparation, then squeeze juice of lemons into preparation. All articles in this preparation should be well mixed together and put in pastry, and baked immediately in a hot oven. Only one layer of pastry at bottom of pie plate.

### 51. Coconut Pie.

One coconut fresh, draw off the milk, then place the nut in a hot oven and let it stay long enough for the shell to pull off; then grate with the nut juice one tea-cup of powdered white sugar, one tablespoonful of butter and lard rubbed together until creamed, then take the yolks of four eggs and beat into sugar and butter until perfectly light; grate the rind of one lemon into it, and squeeze the juice of the lemon into the creamed butter and sugar; beat the white of four eggs light, and add also to creamed butter and sugar, and stir them well, add also one-half tea-cup of sweet milk. Will make three pies. Use a half pound of flour for the pastry, one tablespoonful each of butter and lard—you only want crust at the bottom of plate, and bake in quick oven. Mix flour as directed in No. 49.

### 52. Cream Apple Pie.

The best of apples to be used. To two pounds of apples use a gill of water; put on fire to steam till the apples will mash perfectly fine and soft; sweeten to taste and let them cool. Season with powdered cinnamon—one-half teaspoonful of the best. Have one crust of pastry only, and that at the bottom of plate; fill plate with the fruit, then bake quickly in a hot oven. Take one pint of fresh cream sweetened to taste; beat the white of five eggs light, and add to the cream; flavor with vanilla. Beat the cream lightly before adding the eggs, then with a spoon spread over pies on sending to table.

### 53. Sweet Potato Pie.

Two pounds of potatoes will make two pies. Boil the potatoes soft; peel and mash fine through a colander while hot; one tablespoonful of butter to be mashed in with the potato. Take five eggs and beat the yolks and whites separate and add one gill of milk; sweeten to taste; squeeze the juice of one orange, and grate one-half of the peel into the liquid. One half teaspoonful of salt in the potatoes. Have only one crust and that at the bottom of the plate. Bake quickly.

### 54. Custard Pie.

Half dozen eggs beaten together lightly; one pint of sweet milk; sweeten to taste. Grate one nutmeg in it. Have one crust only, and that at the bottom of plate. Use deep plates and bake quickly. It will make two nice pies.

### 55. Gooseberry and Cherry Pies.

Prepared the same way. Use one gill of water to two pounds of either fruit; sweeten to taste, leaving it a little tart. When it cools, put into plates for baking, having two crusts, top and bottom of plate. Bake quickly, and send to table cold.

### 56. Orange Pie.

Peel the oranges; cut them very thin and spread with sugar thickly. Have your pie crust rich, the same as other pie pastry. Lay bottom crust in plate, and put in the oranges with juice, then cover over with top crust, and put to bake in a quick oven.

### 57. Light Bread Pie.

Take stale bread and grate it. To one and one-half tea-cupfuls of the grated bread, add two tea-cupfuls of sweet milk, the juice of one orange, and half of the peel grated. Stir the yolks of four eggs beaten light into it. Take the whites of the four eggs beaten very light and meringue the pies after baking. Put half tea-cupful of sugar and one tablespoonful of butter to the prepared bread. Have one crust only, and that at the bottom of plate. Bake quickly.

### 58. Cracker Pie.

To be made the same as bread pie, except flavor with one-half teaspoonful of ground cloves, one-half teaspoonful of ground cinnamon, and one tablespoonful of butter.

### 59. Mince Pies.

One beef tongue boiled tender, then take the skin off; four pounds beef kidney suet, peel all the skin off it and chop very fine with the tongue; two pounds citron chopped fine, four pounds apples, four pounds raisins well seeded, four pounds currants well washed and dried with a towel, four oranges, the peel of two grated, and the fruit of all four grated into mince meat, two tablespoonfuls of ground allspice, one tablespoonful of cloves, two nutmegs grated, and two tablespoonfuls of ground cinnamon. Chop the whole very fine, and mix well together, then put in one-half gallon sherry wine, and one-half gallon brandy. Grate two lemons in the meat. Salt to your taste, also sweeten to your taste. Have bottom and top crust.

### 60. Gold Cake.

Take one dozen eggs and separate the yolks from the white, and beat the yolks very light; one pound of butter, one pound of flour and one pound of powdered sugar; rub the butter and sugar together until creamed very light, then add the beaten yolks of the eggs to the creamed butter and sugar, and beat again until light. Take two teaspoonfuls of the best yeast powder, and sift with the one pound of flour, then add this flour to the creamed butter and eggs, with a half tea-cupful of sweet milk, and stir the whole hard and fast till light, then grate the peel of one lemon and squeeze the juice in the cake and stir well.

### 61. Silver Cake.

The whites of one dozen eggs beaten very light, one pound of butter, one pound of powdered sugar; rub the butter and sugar together until creamed very light, then add the beaten whites of the eggs, and beat all together until very light; two teaspoonfuls of the best yeast powder sifted with one pound of flour, then add the flour to the eggs, sugar and butter, also add one-half tea-cupful of sweet milk; mix quickly, and beat till very light; flavor with two teaspoonfuls of the extract of almond or peach, put in when you beat the cake the last time. Put to bake in any shape pan you like, but grease the pan well before you put the cake batter in it. Have the stove moderately hot, so as the cake will bake gradually, and arrange the damper of stove so as send heat to the bottom of the cake first. This instruction of baking applies to all cakes except tea cakes.

### 62. Almond Cake.

Is made in the same way that the silver and gold cakes are, except you take one tea-cup of almonds, scald them in hot water, wipe them with a cloth and the peeling will come off. Either split or chop them fine; suit yourself in this respect. Use the whites or the yolks of one dozen eggs. With the whites of the eggs it will be a silver almond cake; the yolks used alone will be a gold almond cake.

### 63. Feather Cake.

One tea-cup of butter, two of flour, two of sugar. Cream the flour and butter together; two teaspoonfuls of yeast powder to one tea-cup of sweet milk. Mix all with the flour and beat light with a large spoon. To be baked in round tins. Grease well and bake in a moderately hot stove.

### 64. Sponge Cake.

Take one dozen eggs and put in scales as the balance for weighing an equal quantity of sugar. Then balance flour to the weight of six eggs. Beat the yolks of the dozen eggs with the sugar very light, then beat the whites very light and add to the other. Grate the peel of one lemon into it also, squeezing the juice in, and then stir the flour in lightly. Have your pans in readiness, grease with butter, and place white paper at bottom of pan. This should be done for all cakes. A sponge cake should not stand a second after made before it is baked. Bake in a medium oven, keeping heat at bottom.

## 65. Fruit Cake.

One pound of flour sifted and browned in stove, one pound of citron sliced into very small pieces, one pound of raisins cut in small pieces, one pound of currants well washed and dried with clean towel, one tea-cup of almonds chopped fine, one tablespoonful of powdered cinnamon, half a teaspoonful of mace, one tablespoonful of allspice, half a teaspoonful of ground cloves, one pint of black molasses strained before using, one wineglass of brandy, one pound of butter, one pound of sugar, one dozen eggs. Beat whites and yolks separate, light, before adding to cake.

## 66. Jelly Cake.

For this cake make an orange marmalade and use in the place of jelly, as it makes a more delicious cake. Following are the directions: Half a dozen oranges to a tea-cup of granulated sugar; peel oranges and grate them, pick out the seed and pith, add sugar to oranges and stir well and put to cook; stir while cooking; twenty minutes will cook it. It must be made a day before using it for cake. For making the cake, one tea-cup of butter to two of sugar, three of flour and half a dozen eggs. Beat the whites and yolks of eggs separate, very light. Cream butter and sugar together, add the yolks of eggs to creamed sugar and butter, then add the whites, and add flour and stir till light. Sift two teaspoonfuls of best yeast powder with the flour. With the above directions the cake is made. Place it in the pans and put to bake; fifteen minutes will bake it. Spread marmalade over the cake after it is baked. Icing for the cake: Take the whites of four eggs and beat them very light indeed. Add three tablespoonfuls of powdered sugar, beat sugar and eggs together light, and spread on cake while cake is warm. Take one tea-cup of fine grated coconut and sprinkle over cake while icing is soft.

## 67. Carolas.

Five eggs to two cups of sugar; break eggs into the sugar and beat the whole till perfectly light. Sift one quart of flour; take one-half tea-cup of sweet milk and put a level teaspoonful of soda in it, without lumps; one teaspoonful of salt. Flavor with the juice of one orange, the peel of half an orange, grated, and one teaspoonful of butter. Make the dough in the same way as for light bread; roll out dough as for biscuit. Cut them out five inches by two inches, slice them two inches in the middle and stretch open a little. Have your fat boiling hot, but do not let it burn. Put carolas in hot fat, shake skillet gradually till brown. As you take them out of the fat, lay them in a pan on clean paper, so as to drain

## 68. Raised Cake.

One quart flour, half a pound butter, one pint sugar, two eggs, half a tea-cup yeast, one tea-cup seeded raisins, one and one-half tea-cups currants. Cream butter and sugar together, then add the flour. Break eggs in, add yeast and beat the whole well. Lastly, add the fruit, stir all well and put it to rise. With good yeast it will rise in an hour. After rising, make off and put into pans greased with butter. When you make off the second time and put in pans, first take a tablespoonful of flour with a teaspoonful of soda and sift into the batter; it will rise in thirty minutes. Then put to bake.

## 69. Old-Time Ginger Cake.

One pint molasses, one quart flour, one-half tea-cup brown sugar, one tea-cup butter, one tablespoonful cinnamon, two tablespoonfuls ginger, one tea-cup sour milk. With it mix a teaspoonful soda and three eggs. Cream butter and sugar together, then add molasses, then flour, then eggs, then milk, then ginger and cinnamon; stir thoroughly and put to bake in oblong pans.

## 70. Ginger Cookies.

One tea-cup of molasses, one-half tea-cup of sugar, one tablespoonful of butter, one tablespoonful of lard, one quart of flour, two tablespoonfuls of ginger, one teaspoonful of cinnamon, one teaspoonful of allspice, two tablespoonfuls of yeast powder. Cream butter and sugar together and add molasses. Sift yeast powder and flour together and add to butter, sugar and molasses, then add lard and spices, etc., and work it up well. Roll out on a board, and cut them out and bake like you would a biscuit.

## 71. Jumble Cake.

One tea-cup of butter, one and one-half tea-cups of sugar, one and one-half pints of flour; four eggs, two teaspoonfuls of cinnamon, one-half tea-cup of almonds chopped fine, two teaspoonfuls of yeast powder sifted in the flour. Beat the butter, sugar and eggs together, then add the flour. Put cinnamon and almonds in and work the whole up well, then roll on the board to thickness of half an inch, and cut out a finger's length and join together at ends, so as to be round. Grease pans with butter and put to bake.

### 72. Sweet Wafers.

One tea-cup each of butter and sugar creamed together, one grated orange, four eggs, one tablespoonful of cinnamon. Add three pints of flour and make up stiff. Then roll out on a board and cut them out about the size of a biscuit, and roll again till thin as paper, and bake in a quick oven. Watch close while baking. You can roll them round on a fork handle while they are warm, if you like.

### 73. Sweet Cucumber Pickles.

Take as many pickles as you want to make that have already been pickled in vinegar, and slice them in four pieces lengthwise, or cut them crosswise the thickness of a silver half-dollar, and place them in an earthen jar in layers of about three inches in thickness, covering each layer of pickles all over with granulated sugar. Keep repeating the layers three inches thick and covering them with sugar until you have placed all the pickles under sugar you have cut up. Let them remain under the sugar twenty-four hours, then take them out and put them in jars. Then make a syrup in the following way: One quart of sugar to one quart of clear water, and let it boil down to one quart. You will then have one quart of pure syrup. Add one tea-cup of wine vinegar to one pint of syrup, then add the vinegar syrup to the pickles until they are thoroughly covered. Always use granulated sugar.

### 74. Sweet Cucumber Mangoes.

Take large pickled cucumbers, open them with a knife on one side to within half an inch of each end. Scrape out the inside with your fingers, then sprinkle them inside with granulated sugar as thick as a ten-cent piece. Let them remain in that state twenty-four hours or longer, then stuff perfectly full and tie them or wrap with white cord. Make the stuffing in the following way: Take one-fourth of a head of a small cabbage, cut up fine, and two dozen cucumber pickles the size of those to be stuffed. Slice them in small pieces the size of a cherry, and two large onions sliced thin. Then chop fine one dozen cucumber pickles, two pounds of white mustard seed, one tablespoonful of ground allspice, one teaspoonful of ground cloves, sugar to your taste, one-half gallon of wine vinegar. Then put to boil slowly in a porcelain kettle; two hours will cook it. Salt and pepper to your taste. Make syrup in the same way as the sweet pickles in No. 73. You boil a few cloves in the vinegar that is put in the syrup of these pickles, and syrup and vinegar in same way.

### 75. Chow Chow.

Take one cabbage, a large one, and cut up fine. Put in a large jar or keg, and sprinkle over it thickly one pint of coarse salt. Let it remain in salt twelve hours, then scald the cut-up cabbage with one gallon of boiling vinegar. Cut up two gallons of cucumbers, green or pickled, and add to it; cut in pieces the size of the end of little finger. Then chop very fine two gallons more of cucumbers or pickles and add to the above. Seasonings: One pound of brown sugar, one tablespoonful of cayenne pepper, one tablespoonful of black pepper, two gallons of pure wine vinegar, two tablespoonfuls of turmeric, six onions, chopped fine or grated. Then put it on to cook in a large porcelain kettle, with a slow fire, for twelve hours. Stir it occasionally to keep it from burning. You can add more pepper than is here given if you like it hot.

### 76. Creole Chow Chow.

One gallon of green tomatoes, sliced thin, half dozen silver skin onions, sliced thin, one gallon wine vinegar, two tea-cups of brown sugar, one tablespoonful of cayenne pepper, one tablespoonful black pepper, one tablespoonful of turmeric. Put the onions and tomatoes together in a keg or jar and sprinkle over them one pint of salt and let it so remain twenty-four hours, then drain all the brine off from them over colander, then put the vinegar to them and add the seasoning, and put to cook on a slow fire, stir to keep from burning. It will take the whole day to cook; you can make any quantity you want, by doubling the quantity of vegetables and seasonings here prescribed, or if you want a less quantity, lessen the proportion, say half the quantity, then you want a half gallon of tomatoes to begin with, and a half of everything else needed in this chow chow.

### 77. Cherry Chutney.

Get your cherries and seed them; to one gallon half dozen silver skin onions chopped fine; first put the onions to cook in half gallon of vinegar, 10 minutes, then add the cherries, season with two ounces of ground cinnamon, one teaspoonful of cayenne pepper and one of black pepper, two tablespoonfuls of salt, then let it continue to cook with a slow fire, twelve hours, stir it occasionally and keep from burning.

### 78. Game Sauce.

Take one peck of plums, half dozen silver skin onions and chop them very fine; put on the plums to cook. First seed plums; use a porcelain kettle; put the onions to stew in a pint of vinegar until thoroughly done, then add them to the plums; four pounds of granulated sugar to be added; season with one teaspoonful of cayenne pepper, one of black pepper, two ounces of cinnamon broke in fine pieces; cook on a slow fire, stir frequently to avoid burning—one teaspoonful of table salt—it will take one whole day to cook; when cool cork in a tight jar and keep in cool closet—you will find it the best sauce in the world.

### 79. Compound Tomato Sauce.

One peck of ripe tomatoes, cut them in slices and put them in a vessel, and add one tea-cupful of salt to them, two ounces fine allspice, one ounce of fine cloves, one tablespoonful of black pepper and one of cayenne pepper, five large silver skin onions cut up fine, and the whole stand twenty-four hours; mix well together when you set to stand, then put it to cook with one quart of vinegar and let it cook all day; stir it occasionally; it must become thick before it is thoroughly cooked, then strain all skin and studs out of it through a sieve; when cool put in a demijohn, as it is will keep better than in bottles when first made.

N. B. If you don't like much pepper use half the quantity, if you like it very hot use double the quantity.

### 80. Napoleon Sauce.

Twenty green cucumbers to one quart of Chili peppers and one dozen Bell peppers, (take out seeds), and chop the cucumbers and pickles fine, and mix well together, and sprinkle half a tea-cupful of salt over them. Chop half dozen red onions in it. Pour one gallon of vinegar over it and let it stand that way one day and night, then put it to cook next morning and cook slowly all day, stirring it occasionally to keep it from burning, then strain through a sieve. Take a half tea-cupful of brown sugar and put it in a frying pan on the fire, and let it bake thoroughly—just next to burning; then stir in one pint of vinegar to the sugar and when it comes to a light boil strain it through a sieve into the sauce, and stir till well mixed. When cooled cork up in a demijohn.

### 81. Pepper Mangoes.

Take the Bell peppers and scald them in boiling vinegar, then cut the top end of the peppers out and clean out the seeds nicely, as the seeds are no good. You will then prepare a stuffing in the following way: Take one gallon of cucumber pickles, one-half of a head of large cabbage, one-half dozen large silver skin onions, and chop them all up very fine, (the cabbage will chop better if you first slice it thin with a sharp knife): then take two pounds of white mustard seeds, sift all the dust from them and wash clean, one-quarter pound of celery seed, and two quarts of vinegar; add to the vegetables, and put to boil and boil slowly for three hours, stirring it every two or three minutes, Season while cooking with one tablespoonful of cayenne pepper and one of black pepper. If you do not like it very hot, use half the quantity of each kind of pepper; if you like it very hot double the quantity of each kind of pepper. When the stuffing becomes cool, stuff your Bell peppers, using a teaspoon to stuff with, then place the top back on them, and tie nicely with cord, the same way a bundle is tied, and pack them close together in a keg or barrel. This quantity of stuffing will stuff about fifty large Bell peppers. See that they be covered well with vinegar when packed.

### 82. Meat Dressing.

One peck of young carrots grated, one dozen red skin onions grated, one dozen cauliflowers grated; mix the vegetables together and put to cook, adding two gallons of vinegar. Season with two tablespoonfuls of ground black pepper, one tablespoonful of cayenne pepper, and one tea-cupful of salt, stirring it in well. Put one tea-cupful of brown sugar on the fire in a frying pan, and let cook to a dark brown, then pour in two tea-cupfuls of vinegar; stir it well and strain it through a sieve into the kettle while cooking, and let it cook slowly one day. This dressing is nice for all meat entrees, soups and gravies; put two tablespoonfuls to one-half gallon soup, and one tablespoonful to one quart of stew, etc.

### 83. Sweet Pickle Peach.

Use the cling stone peach, taking as many as you may want to pickle. Have your vinegar boiling hot, and drop your peaches into it, letting them remain in the hot vinegar for five minutes, then take them out and put them in a stone jar; about every six inches of peaches cover with sugar one inch thick, putting them in the jar this way—a layer of peaches and then a layer of sugar—until you get all the peaches under sugar. Use five pounds of sugar to ten pounds of peaches. Let the peaches remain under sugar one day, then take the juice that comes out of the peaches, and the sugar if any remain undissolved, and add two pounds more of sugar to it, and put on the fire in a porcelain kettle, and let it cook to a thick clear syrup, then pour the syrup boiling hot over the peaches. Now take the vinegar the peaches were scalded in, and put it to boil the second time, adding while boiling one-half tea-cupful of whole allspice, and one ounce of whole cloves and then pour it on the peaches and boil. Pour this juice on the peaches for nine mornings alternately.

### 84. Sweet Pickle Pears.

Follow the same directions in making sweet pickle pears as in making sweet pickle peaches, as given in Recipe No. 83.

### 85. Sweet Pickle Prunes.

Follow the same directions as given in Recipe No. 83 for making sweet pickle peaches, except use cinnamon bark instead of allspice—one tea-cupful of cinnamon to ten pounds of prunes.

### 86. Sweet Watermelon Rind Pickle.

Take the melon rind and scrape all the meat from the inside, and then carefully slice all the outside of rind from the white part of the rind, then lay or cover the white part over with salt. It will have to remain under salt one week before pickling; the rind will keep in salt from year to year. When you want to pickle it, take it from the salt and put into clear water, change the water three times a day—must be changed say every four hours—then take the rind from water and dry it with a clean cloth. Have your vinegar boiling, and put the rind into it and let it scald four minutes, then take it off the fire and let it lay in vinegar four days; then take it from the vinegar, drain, and sprinkle sugar thickly over it and let it remain so one day. To make syrup, take the syrup from the rind and add eight pounds more sugar to it, and put to boil; boil till a thick and clear syrup. Weigh ten pounds of rind to twelve pounds of sugar; cover the rind with four pounds of it and make the syrup with the remaining eight pounds. While the syrup is cooking add one tea-cupful of white ginger root and the peel of three lemons. When the syrup is cooked, then put the rind into the boiling syrup, and let it cook till you can pass a fork through it with ease, then it is done. When cooled put in jar or bottles with one pint of vinegar to one quart of syrup, thus the pickle is made. See that they be well covered with vinegar and syrup as directed.

### 87. Onion Pickles.

Take as many small onions as you desire to pickle and peel them, then put them in a keg or barrel. Lay down one layer of onions about three inches thick, cover them all over with salt freely; then another layer of onions in the same way and cover with salt, and repeat in this manner until all the onions are covered with salt. Let them remain one or two days, then take the onions out of the salt and put them in clear water, letting them remain in the water long enough to be seasoned with salt to your taste. If very salty, you had better change the first water after three or four hours. Put the onions in a large colander or wire sieve and let the water all drain from them, then put them into a keg, cover them with vinegar, and let them remain in the vinegar twenty-four hours. Take the vinegar from them and put it on to boil, seasoning it with the following spices: Two gallons of vinegar will take one tea-cupful of allspice, two tablespoonfuls of cloves, one-half tea-cupful of black pepper (wash and pick all gravel from the pepper before putting in vinegar), one-fourth pound of white ginger, one-fourth pound of Chile peppers. This seasoning must be boiled in the vinegar, and when boiled twenty minutes, strain vinegar from the spices through a colander on to the pickles, and always prepare enough in this way to have your pickles well covered with vinegar.

### 88. Plain Pickles.

Any vegetable you want to pickle under this head, say small or large cucumbers, cabbage or green tomatoes, have them fresh and put them into a barrel, one layer of cucumbers, or other vegetable, about three inches deep, covering thickly with salt, and repeating layers and salt until you have under brine all you desire to pickle. Let them remain under the brine, if you want to pickle right away, for twenty-four hours, which is long enough, but they will keep a long time by always having them well pressed down with a heavy rock. If you are going to pickle vegetables twenty-four hours after putting them in salt, let them lay in fresh water for two hours, so as to get the smell of the old brine off them. Take them out of the water and put to drain on a sieve made for that purpose of galvanized iron, square, three by four feet, or larger, if needed. Let them drain two or three days, then put in a clean keg or barrel and cover thoroughly with vinegar. Sprinkle over a keg of pickles two ounces of powdered alum while under the vinegar. Let them so remain twelve or twenty-four hours, then pour off the vinegar from the pickles into a large kettle and put to boil. Season while boiling, to five gallons of vinegar, one tea-cupful of allspice, one-fourth pound of ginger root, two ounces of cloves, one-half tea-cupful of black pepper, two tablespoonfuls of cayenne pepper. If you do not like pickles very hot, use one-half the quantity of peppers. When it boils with the seasonings twenty minutes, pour the boiling vinegar over the pickles. Make enough vinegar from these directions to cover well your pickles. They will keep a long time if under vinegar. Sprinkle over a five-gallon keg, when you put the vinegar on the pickles, two or three ounces of powdered alum, if you like pickles brittle.

### 89. Brandy Peaches.

Always have the cling peach, free from decay. Peel the peaches and put down in a jar; one layer of peaches about four peaches deep, covering thickly with granulated sugar; then another layer of peaches covered with sugar, and continue in this manner until you get all the peaches in the jar you wish to brandy. Let them remain under sugar twenty-four hours; then take the same juice that comes from the peaches while under sugar, boil it and pour over the peaches boiling hot. Let them remain in this boiling syrup until it cools. Take this same syrup and put on to boil, adding more sugar so as to make it thick. When it is thoroughly cooked or all sugar is dissolved, put up the peaches in glass jars, and to one tea-cupful of syrup add one tea-cupful of brandy and pour over the peaches, continuing the same proportions of syrup and brandy until the peaches are completely covered with the mixture. Cork the jars and put in closet. You need not seal the jars unless you wish.

### 90. Brandy Peaches—No. 2.

Have the cling peach, free from decay. Peel as in preceding recipe. Weigh the peaches after peeling, or measure them in a gallon measure, so as to allow one pound of sugar to one gallon of peaches in making the syrup. Then put the sugar on the fire to make the syrup, adding enough clear water to keep the sugar from burning while melting. Let the syrup boil until it gets as thick as honey. Put your peeled peaches in a stone jar—one that is air-tight. Set the jar, with the peaches in it, in a kettle on the fire and fill the kettle (not the jar) with cold water. Then take one tea-cupful of syrup to one tea-cupful of brandy and pour it on the peaches until they are covered thoroughly with the brandy and syrup. Let the water in the kettle around the jar of peaches boil for three hours, and no longer. Close the jar up tight, so as to keep the heat in it while boiling. After three hours of actual boiling, lift the kettle with jar in it from the fire, and set aside to cool where a draught of air will not strike it. When thoroughly cool, pack the peaches in glass jars, and fill with brandy and syrup as directed where peaches are boiled. If not enough, use equal proportions of brandy and syrup till the peaches are covered. These brandy peaches are great appetizers, especially for invalids.

### 91. Quince Preserves.

Never use decayed fruit. Put quinces in a kettle of boiling water on the fire, well covered with water, and let boil until they are soft enough to stick a fork into them easily. Then take them off the fire and peel them, cutting them into four pieces and taking all the core out nicely. Put a layer of sugar, then a layer of quinces about six inches deep, then cover thickly with sugar. You must have an equal quantity of sugar and quinces, say pound to pound. Let them remain in sugar a day and night, then put the sugar the quinces were in on to boil, and when it comes to a boil, put the quinces into the syrup. Let them remain in boiling syrup on the fire ten minutes, then take them out and put others in the same syrup, to remain boiling ten minutes. Then put the others back into the syrup again some length of time, and keep repeating the change in this manner for the whole day, as quinces take a whole day to preserve. When they get the color of gold coin they are preserved. Then put them in jars when cold, and put the same syrup on them. If there is not enough syrup to cover them fully, make more syrup. Use granulated sugar with all preserves, and a porcelain kettle for all preserves and pickles.

### 92. Syrups for Preserves.

To ten pounds of sugar add three pints of clear water, hot or cold. When it commences to boil skim the froth from it with a spoon, and let it boil until the froth ceases to collect, then the syrup is made.

### 93. Preserved Peaches.

Have cling peaches, peel them, cut them in half and take the kernels out. Put peaches in sugar, a layer of peaches, then a layer of sugar. Weigh peaches and sugar equally. Each layer of peaches should be about six inches deep; then cover with sugar. Keep repeating sugar and peaches in this manner until you get them all under sugar. Let them remain so one day and night. Next day take sugar and juice from the peaches and put on to boil, and when it comes to a boil, put the peaches in the syrup and let them boil ten minutes. Then take them out and put others in, and when the first lot gets cold put them back into syrup again, and keep repeating in this manner, letting them boil for ten minutes at a time, until preserved. When the peaches look the color of gold coin they are preserved. When they are cold put them in jars, cover with syrup, seal or cork, and set away in a dark closet. Use the syrup they were preserved in; if you have not enough, make more. In preserving any kind of fruit, while cooking always keep the froth well skimmed off top of syrup, and don't neglect it.

### 94. Pear Preserves.

Are to be prepared the same way that peaches are prepared, except in case you want to preserve them whole, then do not cut them into pieces, but only peel them and lay them under sugar in the same manner as the peaches are done, also take one-quarter pound of white ginger root to ten pounds of pears, crack or bruise it, and sprinkle it over each layer of pears, under the sugar; let them remain a day and night, and take the juice and sugar from the pears next day and put to boil for the syrup with the ginger in it; let them boil for ten minutes at a time, and repeat till done; skim the froth off the top of the syrup whenever it appears. When the pears are cold put in jars or bottles and place in a dark closet; they are preserved when they get to the color of gold coin.

If you cannot bruise the ginger root slice it in pieces with a knife and put on pears as directed.

### 95. Currant Jelly.

Be sure and have fresh currants that are not running the juice off. Put the currants in a cloth or bag and squeeze the juice thoroughly from the fruit, then strain the juice through a thin cloth. Measure the juice of the currants; then measure an equal quantity of sugar and place the sugar in a baking pan and put on the stove to heat through thoroughly—it must neither brown nor burn—then put the currant juice and sugar on in a porcelain kettle to boil; it must boil slowly, and whenever the froth or foam gathers on the top of the jelly, skim it all off, so as to let the jelly boil clear. Let the currant juice commence boiling before you put the sugar in, then boil both together for thirty minutes; then dip up some of the jelly and pour it in a saucer and seat in the air: if it congeals in five minutes it is made, if not, let it cook on, and about every ten minutes try it again as before, until it congeals. Have boiling water, and as soon as your jelly is cooked dip your glasses in the boiling water and then turn them upside down long enough for the water to drain out of them. Pour the jelly into the glasses while they are hot, and then seat them in the air to cool with the jelly in them. To paper them after they get cold, have good brandy; cut some thin paper for the inside of the glass and wet it in the brandy, then lay it on the jelly inside of the glass; after covering them put away in a dark place. Use granulated sugar.

### 96. Cranberry Jelly.

Follow the same directions as given in Recipe No. 95 for making currant jelly. Use granulated sugar.

### 97. Strawberry Jam.

Must have fresh berries that are not running. Squeeze the juice from the berries through a clean linen cloth; then add one-half pint of sugar to every pint of juice and put on to boil in a porcelain kettle, and when it boils as thick as honey add the berries that you squeezed the juice from to the syrup and let it continue to boil until it gets as thick as mush, when it will be cooked enough. You can put it up in glasses or jars; put paper on the top wet with brandy, and then cover and put in a dark place. Use granulated sugar.

### 98. Raspberry and Currant Jam combined.

Take an equal quantity of both kinds of fruit and squeeze the juice from them; measure the juice and put one pint of it to one-half pint of sugar; then put on to boil, letting it boil till thick as honey; then add the berries and currants that you squeezed the juice from, and let all boil together till thick as mush, when it will be cooked. Put up in bowls, jars or glasses, covering inside with paper wet in brandy, and then put away in a dark place. Use granulated sugar.

### 99. Marmalade Peach.

Peel the peaches and take the seeds away. Use the freestone peach, taking one-half pound of sugar to one pound of peaches. Sprinkle the sugar thickly over the peaches and let them lay in the sugar one night; next morning mash the peaches and sugar thoroughly, and put to cook, and let it cook slowly. Do not put any water to it. It requires five hours cooking. Use porcelain kettle and keep from burning. Use granulated sugar. Can be put up in glasses, jars or bowls.

### 100. Crab Apple Jelly.

Put the apples to boil; one quart of water to one quart of apples and let them boil till soft; then mash the apples and put the apples and the water they were boiled in a linen rag, and let all the juice drip into a vessel; measure the juice and take one quart of the dripped juice to one quart of sugar, and put on to boil for jelly. Boil thirty minutes and then dip some into a saucer and set in the air to cool; if it is congealed when cool, it is done. Put up in glasses, first dipping the glasses into boiling hot water and letting them drain; put the jelly into the glasses hot, and then set to cool. Paper the same way you do currant jelly, and put away in a dark place. Use a porcelain kettle and granulated sugar.

### 101. Blackberry Brandy.

To five gallons of berries add one gallon of the best brandy; put on fire in a porcelain kettle and let it just come to a boil, then take it off the fire and make a syrup of granulated sugar; ten pounds of sugar to one quart of water. Let the syrup cook till thick as honey, skimming off the foam while boiling; then pour it upon the brandy and berries and let it stand eight weeks; then put in bottle or demijohn. This blackberry brandy took a diploma at the State Fair of 1879. Let the berries, brandy and syrup stand in a stone jar or brandy keg for eight weeks when you take it off the fire.

### 102. Blackberry Syrup—For Dysentery in children.

Take one quart of berries and mash up fine in a bowl squeezing all the juice from them, then strain the juice through a thin muslin cloth. To this juice add one pound of crushed sugar and put to boil in a porcelain saucepan, adding one ounce of whole clove and one-half ounce of cinnamon, tying the cinnamon up in a clean cloth; let the cloves remain in the syrup ever after is cooked. It will take two hours steady boiling to cook. Put into bottles when cool. Dose for an infant of six months, a teaspoonful three times a day till bowels are checked. For a grown person one-half wine glass three times a day. This recipe is an old Southern plantation remedy among colored people.

### 103. Preserved Apricots.

Weigh an equal quantity of sugar and apricots, or if you are going to preserve fifty pounds of apricots weigh fifty pounds of sugar, take the sugar and put it in a porcelain kettle the day before you buy the apricots, put two gallons of water at bottom of sugar in kettle, let it boil until thick as honey, seat off fire; next day you get the apricots, put the syrup again on the fire and have it boiling before you drop the apricots in; take the apricots out of boiling syrup every five minutes and put others in boiling syrup to remain boiling five minutes and take out before those last in; repeat the shifting of the apricots every five minutes for five hours when they will be preserved. If you want to preserve a less quantity you can do so; the only instructions needed is, to one pound of apricots one pound of sugar; make syrup the day before getting the apricots and set aside, the next day boil it and put apricots in while boiling. For making syrup, to one pound of sugar half pint of water.

### 104. Apple Sauce for Roast Pork.

One dozen apples cut very thin, put them in half pint of boiling water, in a nice white saucepan, add a little sugar according to taste.

### 105. Charlotte Russe.

One pint of sweet cream to four eggs; three tablespoonfuls of sugar; Beat first the whites of the eggs to a light froth; then beat the cream to a light froth; then beat the sugar in the eggs; then beat two additional tablespoonfuls of sugar in the cream, light; then add the cream and eggs together; flavor with one and a half teaspoonful of best vanilla, and stir well; then lay your cakes, lady fingers, in the mould, well at the bottom and close together around the sides; then pour in the russe on the cake and set in the ice box it is made. See that mould is in perfect order. To be served on table with teaspoons on small saucers.

Use granulated sugar in all sweets.

### 106. Ice Cream.

One quart of sweet cream and the whites of six eggs beaten to a light froth; then beat in the eggs half tea-cup of sugar. Beat the cream light, and add one tea-cupful of sugar to cream and beat again until light, flavor with one and a half tablespoonful of vanilla, and put the whole in freezer. Put at the bottom of freezer pail a layer of ice, cover with salt, set freezer in on it and fill in around freezer with ice and salt; a layer of ice and layer of salt until full to the top of freezer; let no salt get inside of freezer. Ten minutes will freeze it.

### 107. Orange Sherbet.

Squeeze the juice from two dozen oranges, add to this one and a quarter pound of fine sugar; stir well and freeze the same way as in ice cream.

### 108. Lemon Sherbet.

Squeeze the juice from one dozen lemons; add two quarts of water and one and a half pounds of lump sugar; let sugar dissolve and stir well, and freeze the same way as in ice cream.

### 109. Pine Apple Sherbet.

Cut in slices two pine apples, early in the morning, and lay them in one and one-half pounds of fine sugar for three hours. Squeeze all the juice from the apple and put to freeze like ice cream.

### 110. Snow Pudding.

One whole box of Cox's gelatin to a pint of cold water and let it remain one hour; then pour a quart of boiling water on it. Beat the whites of ten eggs to a light froth, and add one and one-half tea-cupfuls of granulated sugar. When the gelatin gets cold add one-half tea-cupful of sugar and the juice of one lemon. Beat gelatin into the eggs light. Beat the yolks of ten eggs into one tea-cupful of sugar; boil one pint of rich milk and pour it boiling on the beaten eggs, stirring well. After this custard cools, add one glass of sherry wine, and set aside for dessert, to be eaten with sponge cake. Flavor the gelatin with the juice of one lemon.

### 111. Plum Pudding.

Brown one pound of flour in the stove and sift it three times; add two pounds of stale light bread grated. After cutting the crust (which is not to be used), add one quart of dark molasses to one pint of brown sugar, two grated nutmegs, one tablespoonful of allspice, one tablespoonful of ground cloves, two pounds of citron sliced one-half inch thick, two pounds of currants, two pounds of chopped seeded raisins, one tablespoonful of salt, one and one-half tablespoonfuls of yeast powder, two pounds of beef kidney suet, chopped fine, and taking all strings out of suet. Add all together and stir until thoroughly mixed. Have a bag made in the shape of a sugar-loaf and wet it in cold water, sprinkling on the inside thickly with flour. Put the pudding in the bag and let it boil for seven hours, tie the bag securely.

Sauce for this plum pudding: One pint of white sugar to two tablespoonfuls of butter and one claret glass of good brandy, and put to boil till thick as honey, and serve with pudding, hot.

### 112. Boiled Turkey.

See that the turkey is well cleaned. If you like high seasoning, one teaspoonful of cayenne pepper on the inside and one tablespoonful of salt on the outside. Season with two teaspoonfuls of black pepper. If you do not like high seasoning, one-half the quantity of salt and pepper will do. Let it lay in this salt and pepper one hour before boiling, then have enough raw ham and veal to thoroughly stuff the turkey in the craw and body. Chop the veal and ham fine together before stuffing the turkey. Season with one-half teaspoonful of salt and one-half teaspoonful of cayenne pepper, then add one dozen oysters to stuffing, sprinkling a teaspoonful of dry mustard and half a tea-cupful of browned crackers, powdered. Work it well with a spoon, stuff the turkey (craw and body) full and tight; Then put the turkey in a bag and tie it very tight, and put on in boiling water sufficient to cover it. Let a young turkey boil an hour and five minutes, and an old turkey two hours. Put one tablespoonful of salt in the water.

For this turkey make a rich drawn butter gravy as follows: Two tablespoonfuls of butter and one and one-half tablespoonfuls of flour. Rub the flour and butter together until well mixed, sprinkling half a teaspoonful of mustard into it. To this add one pint of boiling milk and stir till it is as thick as honey. Put in half a teaspoonful of salt and send gravy to table with the turkey.

### 113. Beef a la Mode.

Take a ten-pound round of beef (have the butcher lard it), and tie it tight with a strong cord. Rub into the beef one and one-half tablespoonfuls of salt, one teaspoonful each of cayenne and black pepper. Have a pot of sufficient size and put the beef into it. Then slice thin four large carrots and two white turnips and lay them around the beef. Put in the pot about four sprigs of parsley, half a pint of good claret, and one small onion, sliced. Let it cook slowly five or six hours and send to table.

### 114. Spiced Round.

A twenty pound round of beef. Rub into this beef, one tea-cup of salt, two tablespoonfuls of cayenne and one of black peppers, quarter pound each of ground allspice and cloves rubbed into beef; then lay the round of beef into a vessel that will fit it and pour two quarts of vinegar on it and let it lay in vinegar one week, turning it over once every day, keeping it covered tight, so as to keep the flavor in it; after one week put it in a kettle to cook. First, tie it up tight in a clean cloth; put all the juice that lay around the beef in to cook with it, adding two quarts of water, and let it boil four hours and a quarter. Let it be cold when it is taken out of the cloth. Slice thin when it is served, as it is excellent for luncheons, parties, etc. The most delicious appetizer among meats.

### 115. Stuffed Ham.

First boil the ham; then take the skin from it while boiling, put one tea-cup of vinegar to it; then take half pound of cooked veal, one tea-cup of powdered cracker; chop veal fine, mix both together, salt and pepper to taste; then make gashes about one-inch a part in the ham; stuff with veal and cracker, and put to bake; then pour one pint of sherry wine over ham and baste the ham while baking, until brown; while ham is baking grate one nutmeg over it, and sprinkle cracker powder over it.

### 116. Baked Fish.

See that fish is well cleaned; then salt and pepper it inside and out, two or three hours before stuffing it or baking. For the stuffing, grate stale bread enough to fill the fish, then put it on fire in a skillet, and add one tablespoonful of butter and one of lard, chop fine one slice of onion and four sprigs of parsley; season with pepper and salt; let the stuffing stay five or ten minutes, stirring it to keep from burning; then stuff the fish until it is perfectly full. Sow it up with a needle and thread and put it to bake in a medium hot stove; pour about half a tea-cup of water in bottom of pan when you put fish on; while fish is baking, baste or spread a little butter on top of fish until it browns, when it will be ready for table.

### 117. Boiled Fish.

See that fish is well cleaned. Season inside and out with pepper and salt one or two hours before putting to boil, then have your boiler with one quart of lukewarm water to receive the fish, and let it remain on a quick fire twenty minutes; if it is a very large fish it will take thirty minutes to cook.

### 118. Sauce for Boiled Fish or Boiled Mutton.

One and a half tablespoonfuls of flour, and one of butter rubbed together until creamed; boil one gill of sweet milk, then add it gradually to this creamed butter and flour, and stir it as you add it, until it is thoroughly mixed; season with pepper and salt to taste. Boil four eggs hard and slice them in four pieces, lengthways, and put the eggs around the dish when you take up the fish to send to table, and also garnish the dish with parsley.

### 119. Jumberlie—A Creole Dish.

Take one chicken and cut it up, separating every joint, and adding to it one pint of cleanly-washed rice. Take about half a dozen large tomatoes, scalding them well and taking the skins off with a knife. Cut them in small pieces and put them with the chicken in a pot or large porcelain saucepan. Then cut in small pieces two large pieces of sweet ham and add to the rest, seasoning high with pepper and salt. It will cook in twenty-five minutes. Do not put any water on it.

### 120. Chicken Salad.

Take all the meat from the bones of a boiled chicken and chop it fine in a tray. Save out some of the breast meat so as to lay over the top of the salad when it is made. Chop fine half a bunch of white celery and add to chicken. Season the chicken with pepper and salt, using cayenne pepper to taste. Skim the oil from the boiling chicken to pour over the salad. Milanese sauce for chicken salad: Beat the yolks of three eggs a little, then add one pint of best sweet oil, beating a little sweet oil at a time into the eggs, so as to have it light, until the whole pint is added. Mix a teaspoonful of mustard thoroughly in strong vinegar and put in sauce with cayenne and black pepper to suit the taste. When you put the salad on the platter, pour this sauce all over it and set it in an ice box.

### 121. Veal Salad.

Make veal salad and sauce in the same manner as chicken salad and sauce.

### 122. Lamb Salad.

Lamb salad is also made in the same manner as chicken salad.

### 123. Shrimp Salad.

Make in the same manner as above, slicing celery and adding to it.

### 124. Crab Salad.

This is also made with the addition of celery sliced into it in very thin pieces, instead of chopping celery.

### 125. Meat Salads.

For any meat salads you desire to make, follow the same directions given for chicken salad.

### 126. Terrapin Stew.

Always have the female terrapins, and put them alive in boiling water. Let them remain for fifteen minutes and then take the shells from them, being careful not to break the galls. Clean the entrails from the meat, and scrape the black skin from the feet with a knife. Half a dozen terrapins will serve twelve persons. After thoroughly cleaning the terrapins, lay them in clear water for ten minutes, and then put them in a kettle to stew with half a pint of water, and stew very slowly for about three hours. Boil half a dozen eggs hard, and rub the yolks to a powder. Then add half a pound of best butter to the eggs and beat together until it becomes a cream. To this cream add one pint of sherry wine and mix it well. Then add this preparation to the stew very gradually, stirring well, so as to thoroughly mix it in. While the stew is cooking, mix a teaspoonful of best mustard to a tablespoonful of wine and put in. Slice one lemon and add to stew just before dishing it up for table. Three hours is sufficient time to cook it. You had better put the wine in the stew and not mix it with the eggs, for fear you may not mix it in right and that there may be no mistake. With the above directions you have a perfect stew, A tea-cupful of sweet cream is an improvement, if you like it; also a dozen grains of allspice. Salt and pepper to taste.

### 127. Fish Chowder.

Cut up one pound of salt pork in pieces one and two inches in size for a large fish, of about six pounds. Cut the fish in pieces the same as the pork; slice in pieces half dozen Irish potatoes the size of fish. Beat one sea cracker fine, take and slice one large onion, chop it fine; fry the pork brown, take it from the fat. Having all now prepared, put your pot on fire, and put in pot a layer of fish, then a layer of pork, then a layer of cracker, then put in one tablespoonful of butter, cayenne pepper, and salt to taste; add one pint of water, and let it stew one hour, when it will be ready for table use.

### 128. Clam Chowder.

Prepare and make clam chowder in the same way as the fish chowder, except you must use tomatoes; a layer of tomatoes and a layer of the other articles, for fifty to one hundred clams. Put in one pint of sweet milk; before putting clams in pot cut away the black part of clams, add half a teaspoonful of ground cloves, and one teaspoonful of ground allspice, salt and pepper to taste; one dozen tomatoes scalded in boiling water, and skin them.

### 129. Creole Soup.

Take three pints of this same bouillon, put on to boil, just before use chop four leaves of parsley fine, and put in. Brown a teaspoonful of brown sugar on a tin plate, add a sherry wine-glass of sherry wine to sugar, stir it well, then strain through a fine sieve; then stir three tablespoonfuls into soup. Beat two yolks of eggs into tureen and pour hot soup on it and send to table.

### 130. Spiced Currants.

Five pounds fresh currants to three pounds of sugar, one pint of vinegar; wash currants and drain all water from them through sieve or colander, add sugar and vinegar to currants, and put to cook in a porcelain kettle; season with one ounce ground cloves and one ounce of stick cinnamon, let it cook gradually until it becomes like a jelly; when it gets cold, put away in bottles and cork tight. Use granulated sugar.

### 131. Spiced Cherries.

Five pounds of cherries to three quarter pounds of sugar, one pint of best vinegar, quarter pound of cloves, quarter pound of allspice. Put sugar, spices and vinegar, all together on fire and boil it, then pour it boiling on the cherries. Before boiling vinegar, spices, and sugar, let cherries lay in spiced vinegar and sugar twenty-four hours, then boil and pour on cherries, and when they get perfectly cold, put up in bottles and cork well.

### 132. Preserved Peaches.

Always preserve the cling peach and none other. Cut your peaches in two or four pieces just as you like, and have one pound of granulated sugar to one pound of peaches; that is to say, if you are going to preserve ten pounds of peaches have ten pounds of sugar, and put the sugar on peaches the day before preserving; then next day pour juice off peaches and put juice on to boil, when it boils, put the peaches in this boiling juice, let them stay five minutes, take them out and lay them on a dish for five minutes, then put them back in the boiling syrup again for five minutes, and repeat or continue taking them out and putting them back every five minutes, for one hour, when they will be preserved.

### *133. Preserved Cherries.*

Seed your cherries and put sugar on them the day before preserving. When you pour off the juice next day and put it to boil, when it boils put cherries in, let them stay five minutes, take them out, put them back in boiling syrup in five minutes, and so continue every five minutes for one hour, when they will be preserved. When preserves are cold put away.

### *134. Corn Fritters.*

To one dozen ears of corn add three eggs, half a tea-cupful of powdered crackers, one tablespoonful of sifted flour. Cut off the corn very lightly from the cob—say half of the grain—and then scrape the other half clean off with a knife. Add the crackers to corn and beat together light. Beat the eggs light and add with the flour and a quarter of a tea-cupful of sweet milk. Season to taste and beat the whole light. Have your lard or butter hot when you go to fry, and drip the batter into the hot fat from off the end of a spoon, letting it fry quick and brown. Have young and tender corn. The fat ought to be hot enough to brown the fritters in two minutes.

### *135. Corn Pudding.*

Take one dozen ears of corn and grate from the cob. Beat four eggs light and add a pint of sweet milk and a tablespoonful of butter, salting and peppering to taste. Beat lightly, place in a deep dish and bake in a hot oven. Ten minutes will bake it. Grease the dish with butter before putting pudding into it, and send to table in the dish it is baked in.

### *136. Carving Poultry.*

In carving always have a sharp knife. First pass the knife close to the body of the fowl, just under the joint of the wing. Then press it back towards the neck with the back of the knife, when it will separate from the body. Take the same course with the leg, and when you have the wings and legs unjointed, turn the fowl on its back and slice meat from the breast and sides, thinly.

### 137. Boiled Corn.

Always put the corn on in boiling water and salt, cooking for seven minutes; a longer cooking than this will take all the sweetness from the corn.

### 138. Apple Roll.

To one quart of flour add a tablespoonful each of butter and lard (or two of butter, if preferred,) and one teaspoonful of fine salt. Work the lard or butter into the flour dry until it is thoroughly mixed, then add salt and a tea-cupful of water, a little at a time, and mix until the dough is sufficiently thick to roll on the pastry block. Always sprinkle dry flour on the block to keep the dough from sticking. Use one and one-half pounds of mellow apples, peeled and cut very thin. Roll your dough out as thin as pie crust, eighteen by ten inches in size. Have three pieces of this size, and lay one sheet of it down and cover it with apples; then lay the second and third sheets down, covering each with apples. Roll the whole up together as you would a towel, then wet a white cloth in cold water and wrap it around the roll, sewing it tightly; then put into a pot of boiling water. Sprinkle dry sugar over each layer of apples before rolling in the cloth. Do not cook over twenty minutes. Put in water enough to cover the roll.

### 139. Sauce for this Roll.

Two tablespoonfuls of butter and one and one-half tea-cupfuls of powdered sugar rubbed together until as light as cream, one-half of a grated nutmeg, one wine-glassful of brandy beaten into the creamed butter and sugar.

### 140. Stuffed Tomatoes.

Cut off the tops of tomatoes, hollow the inside, and mix the inside that you take out with chopped up ham; bread crumbs or crackers powdered, butter, salt and pepper to your taste. Stuff the tomatoes full and replace the top close. Put them in a pan to bake in a hot oven for fifteen minutes.

### 141. Blackberry Roll.

Make this roll by the same directions given for the apple roll.

### 142. Egg Plant Stuffed.

Take out the inside of the plant and boil it in just enough water to cover it for ten minutes, and then drain or press the water all out through a colander. Chop some ham fine, take bread crumbs and butter (one tablespoonful to one egg plant), and have equal proportions of ham, cracker and bread crumbs to the inside of the plants. Season with salt and black pepper to taste and fry it brown. Then stuff the plants full and close and put them to bake. They will bake in ten minutes, but should not be put in the oven until just before table use. They are a delicious vegetable prepared in this manner. Use a hot oven.

### 143. Peach Cobbler.

Peel the peaches (freestones) and make a pastry the same way as for pie, and roll out the dough as thin as for pie crust. Put one layer at the bottom of the dish, and cut the peaches into pieces the size of a plum and fill the dish with them, sprinkling them freely with fine sugar. Cover them over with another layer of pastry, cut with a knife two or three air-holes on the top and put to bake. Let it bake brown. It makes a delicious luncheon or dessert. Season the peaches with powdered cinnamon to taste. See recipe for all kinds of pastry.

### 144. Ladies' Custard.

Boil a quart of sweet milk, and beat together half a dozen eggs with two tablespoonfuls of sugar until light. Pour the milk on the eggs and sugar, stirring well. Put a tablespoonful of sugar into a kettle that will hold the milk and eggs, and let the sugar brown. Then pour the milk and eggs into the kettle and let it come to a boil. Put your custard cups in a baking pan and fill the pan with cold water. Then fill the cups with custard and set in the stove until it becomes as thick as batter. It will need no flavoring extracts.

### 145. Batter Pudding.

Five eggs; beat yolks and whites separately, very light, six tablespoonfuls of flour to one pint of milk, one teaspoonful of salt; sift flour three times, pour half of the milk to the flour and beat it light, then add the beaten yolks of eggs to flour and milk, and then add the whites also and beat again; lastly add the remaining half pint of milk and beat the whole pudding until very light. Have a good, tight, strong white bag, wet it, and put flour thickly on the inside, put pudding in it, tie it tight and put in a pot of boiling water and let it boil three quarters of an hour. Make a sauce of sugar and butter, rub the two together until light, flavor with nutmeg, and stir a wine glass of sherry wine or brandy in it well. Use powdered sugar.

### 146. Baked Batter Pudding.

Use the same directions and quantities as given in the boiled pudding, and when you have it mixed as directed, and have a hot oven, pour pudding in baking pan and bake brown.

### 147. Corned Beef Hash.

Take boiled corned beef and chop it very fine, four hot boiled Irish potatoes to one pound of beef, mash potatoes in the beef while hot, one slice of onion chopped with meat, half a teaspoonful of mustard mixed, two sprigs of parsley; then make into pones like a small loaf of bread, and bake brown. Season with black pepper to taste.

### 148. Tonic Bitters.

A Southern Remedy for Invalids.

Take one ounce of cardamom seed, one ounce of Peruvian bark bruised, two ounces of Gentian root bruised, half ounce of dry orange peel, one ounce of aloes, and put the whole into half a gallon of best whiskey or brandy; let it come to a boil, then strain or filter it through a fine cloth or filtering paper.

Dose half wineglass full three times a day before meals. Will strengthen and produce an appetite.

### 149. Suet Pudding.

One pound of beef kidney suet, chop it fine, taking all strings from it, one pound of flour rubbed into suet until thoroughly mixed, salt to taste; one and a half teaspoonful of yeast powder mixed in with the flour; mix the whole gradually with water, the same way that you mix up dough for any other bread, stiff; then roll out the dough about half an inch thick, and spread the dough with currant jelly; then roll up the dough round like a bottle and as you roll continue to spread the under part of dough with jelly, so as to have all of dough covered with the jelly when it is rolled up finally, then take a clean linen towel and wrap the roll in it tight, sewing the ends and sides well; when you have finished rolling it up in the towel, put it on in boiling water, well covered, and let it boil thirty minutes.

### 150. Sauce for Suet Pudding.

One tablespoonful of butter, one tea-cup of white sugar; rub both together until well mixed to a cream, then put on a kettle over steam, and as it heats stir it until a foam, then add one wine-glassful of brandy; stir until mixed, and flavor with nutmeg, and send to table hot with the pudding.

### 151. Chicken Gumbo.

Salt and pepper chicken before frying it. Take a chicken, separating it from all the joints and breaking the bones, fry the chicken in one and a half tablespoonful of lard or butter. First well mix the chicken in dry flour, let the fat be hot, put chicken to fry until brown; don't burn chicken. After fried, put it on in soup kettle with half a gallon of hot water, one and a half quarts of green ochre cut into thin pieces, throwing the end away, and let the whole boil to three pints; season with pepper and salt. Chop half of an ordinary sized onion fine, and fry it with chicken; chili pepper chopped fine if added is nice when liked.

### 152. Circuit Hash.

One dozen tomatoes, one quart of butter beans, one dozen ears of corn cut off from cob, quarter pound of lean and fat pork cut in fine pieces, if pork is not liked, use two tablespoonfuls of butter; put on in a sauce-pan and stew one hour.

Note. Five minutes before dinner put in the corn to cook with the rest of stew.

### 153. Stewed Tomatoes.

First scald the tomatoes in boiling water and then peel the skin from them, then cut them up in small pieces, cutting also one slice of onion fine in them; add no water; bread crumbs, one tablespoonful of butter, pepper and salt to taste. To one dozen of tomatoes, half a tea-cupful of bread crumbs.

### 154. Rice Pudding.

Two tablespoonfuls of butter and sweeten to taste, one pint of rice boiled soft; thoroughly mix to this rice one pint of rich milk. Beat up two eggs very light, and add to the above also; well mix the whole. Flavor with the grated rind or peel of the half of an orange, and the juice of two oranges; mix well into pudding, and put into pan to bake.

### *155. Meringue for Pudding.*

The whites of five eggs beat very light, four tablespoonfuls of sugar, mix into eggs and beat light; spread thickly over pudding and put to brown.

### *156. Leaven Biscuit.*

Save a piece of leaven from the light bread you mix or make up over night, the size of a tea-cup; mix leaven up soft in water, add half a pint of flour to it, one teaspoonful of salt, seat to rise over night. Next morning take one level quart of flour, pat a level teaspoonful of soda and sift it; rub into this flour one tablespoonful of lard, half tablespoonful of butter, until thoroughly mixed; then add the whole together, and work it with the hands until light, and make off in biscuits and put to rise in baking pan twenty minutes, then bake brown.

### *157. Oyster Pie.*

Make pastry according to directions of pastry for all kinds of pies in receipt No. 48. Have bottom and top crust—bottom crust to be thick as a quarter dollar Then put oyster liquor or juice on in a kettle to boil, and when it boils, skim the foam from it; then drop oysters into boiling liquor for four minutes only, take out oysters, lay them on a dish, then sift two tablespoonfuls of flour, take two tablespoonfuls of butter, rub into flour until well mixed, then dissolve the same with a little of hot liquor, salt and pepper to taste. Then pour into boiling liquor the mixture of flour and butter, stirring the same while pouring it in, till all is poured in. To be baked in a deep pan. Put bottom crust covering bottom and sides of pan, then pour liquor in on crust; when this is done, put the oysters into the pan and cover the pan over with a thick cover of pastry, the thickness of a half dollar, cutting small spaces in several parts on top, the width of a knife blade, and put to bake brown. Take the white of an egg, beat it up and baste top of pie when you put it to bake. One quart of oysters and the juice will make pie for six in family.

### *158. Yorkshire Pudding.*

To be eaten with Roast Beef.

Sift one pint of flour and add to it one-half pint of milk; beat milk into flour with a large spoon until very light; then beat four eggs yolks and whites together very light, and add to flour and milk, and then beat the whole, adding one tablespoonful of butter, salt to taste. Put to bake in a dish; twenty minutes will bake it. When done send to table with roast beef, in same dish it is baked in.

### 159. Cheese Pudding.

Have mild cheese; grate half pound of cheese and half pound of apples, add to this half pint of sweet milk, beat four eggs very light, and add to the above. Before mixing apples with cheese, put to it one tablespoonful of white sugar; stir all well. Season with nutmeg, and pour it into a dish and put to bake, putting one tablespoonful of butter over it in small pieces. Twenty minutes will bake it, and send to table as a vegetable.

### 160. Pap for Infant Diet.

Take one pint of flour, sift it and tie it up in a clean cloth securely tight, so that no water can get into it; and put it in boiling water and let it boil steady for two hours, then take it out of water, and when it gets cold take outside crust from it. Whenever you are ready to nurse or feed the child, grate one tablespoonful of the boiled flour, and stir it into half a pint of boiled milk while the milk is boiling; sweeten the same with white sugar to taste. When the child has diarrhea, boil a two-inch stick of cinnamon in the pap. I have given birth to eleven children and raised them all, and nursed them with this diet. It is a Southern plantation preparation.

### THE END

CPSIA information can be obtained
at www.ICGtesting.com
Printed in the USA
LVHW050329210922
728910LV00002B/180